Making Waves
The Quick Sketch Collection
Stephen Deal

Nimbus Press

COPYRIGHT

We are mainly interested in providing resources for churches that want to use drama in worship, in bible study and in evangelism, and for Amateur Dramatic Groups. **You are free to perform any of our plays and sketches and do not need permission but we would appreciate receiving news of any productions.** **All our plays are protected by copyright and so we ask that you buy copies for each actor when you purchase one.** We hope that you will find them useful for the work of the Kingdom.

Fees for performances by professional companies will be subject to negotiation.

Published by Nimbus Press,
18 Guilford Road, Leicester, LE2 2RB.
Cover illustration by Polly Deal and John Parker.

Copyright © Stephen Deal 1999

British Library Cataloguing in Publication
Data available

ISBN 1 874424 22 5

Printed in Great Britain by
Attwood Dawes Printers, Canon Place,
Eskdaill Street, Kettering, NN16 8RE.

Contents

Introduction

Stephen Deal provided the drama and performance poetry for *Hopes and Dreams* which has enjoyed a sell-out tour to 60,000 people. This presentation of the Lords Prayer for the Millennium has involved around 4500 people in local casts and choirs for each performance. Almost 1000 Churches plan to perform *Hopes and Dreams* in their own communities around the U.K..

Nimbus Press are delighted to offer 15 biblical sketches by Stephen in his first book of sketches.

Stephen believes that Christian drama should entertain as well as containing a 'message'. People must be able to enjoy it.

But drama is also memorable. So get it right and you have sown a seed for a generation. Many Christians agree that Stephen has got it right and we are confident you will have fun reading these sketches and be able to use them profitably in your churches. Like all other Nimbus plays and sketches they are 'Tried and Tested' and you will find them easy to perform.

No Kidding

Characters

Narrator 1
Narrator 2
Lamb
Shepherd

Bible Background

Parable of the sheep and the goats.   Matthew 25.31-46

The actors playing the parts of the lamb and the shepherd could also give the two narrators' readings.

Narr.1   It says in the bible ...

Narr.2   In the book of Matthew ...

Narr.1   That when the Son of Man comes in his glory, and all his angels with him he will sit on his throne in heavenly glory.

Narr.2   All the nations will be gathered before him, and he will separate the people one from another as a shepherd separates the sheep from the goats.

Narr.1   He will put the sheep on his right and the goats on his left.

The officious looking shepherd stands with a crook and a clipboard in the centre of the acting area.. The lamb (wearing a woolly hat?) attempts to get past the shepherd.

Shepherd Oy! Where do you think you're going?

Lamb   I was following the others.

Shepherd As you may or may not be aware The Great Shepherd has determined that in accordance with the decree laid out in M.A.T.T. section twenty five, subsections thirty-one through forty-six, creatures what is determined as being sheep shall traverse to the right and them what is determined as being goats shall traverse to the left.

Lamb   Okay.

Shepherd So before you may proceed we needs to determine whether you are the kind of creature what goes to the left or the kind of creature what goes to the right. Well?

Lamb   What's the difference?

Shepherd The difference is the difference between lying down in green pastures beside still waters, and lying down to spend an indeterminate amount of time at gas mark nine.

Lamb   I'll take the green pastures please.

Shepherd Then you has to be a sheep. Are you a gregarious woolly ruminant of the genus Ovis? Or are you a frisky horned ruminant of the genus Capra?

Lamb   I don't know.

Shepherd Well before you may proceed we must ascertain this critical information.

Lamb   How do we do that?

Shepherd You must answer some questions.

Lamb   Ooh great! A quiz. Go on ask me a question. Any question. I'm great at that Trivial Pursuit.

Shepherd These questions come directly from the Great Shepherd.

Lamb   Fine. Fire away.

Shepherd He asks, "When I was hungry and thirsty, did you feed me?"

Lamb   Me? Me feed the Great Shepherd? I'm not even sure what he looks like. No, I've never fed him.

Shepherd The Great Shepherd asks, "When I was cold did you clothe me?"

Lamb   I've never seen him. How could I have given him something to wear?

Shepherd "When I was in prison did you come and visit me?"

Lamb I didn't even know there had been a trial.

Shepherd That's another no, is it? Oh dear, I smell pot roast.

Lamb This isn't fair. If I'd known the Great Shepherd was hungry or thirsty, or cold or in prison, of course I would have helped him. He's the Great Shepherd, the big cheese, el supremo, the man, the boss. Anyone would have stopped and lent him a hand.

Shepherd Apparently not. Off to the left with you.

Lamb I'm all upset now.

Shepherd I don't make the rules.

The Lamb starts to move slowly away to the left of the shepherd.

Lamb 'Bye then.

Shepherd Good bye.

Lamb I'm off now.

Shepherd Right.

Lamb See you around then.

Shepherd I doubt it.

Lamb Good bye.

The Lamb rushes back and throws itself on its knees

Lamb Please don't make me go. Please.

Shepherd I'm sorry, rules is rules.

Lamb But if I'd known the Great Shepherd was in trouble I would have helped. I promise I would have.

Shepherd Off you go. Just keep bearing left.

The Lamb dejectedly moves away

7

Lamb   I wish I'd kept an eye out for the Great Shepherd instead of spending time with those other people now.

Shepherd What other people?

Lamb   Oh just some poor homeless bloke. I gave him some of my cheese to eat and some wool to make a blanket with. And there was a child who was lost. I helped him find his way home. I must have missed the Great Shepherd while I was busy.

Shepherd Let me just check the regulations.

Lamb   And now I'm going to be doing a guest slot in an Oxo advert. It's time to slam in the Lamb. Oh well ...

Shepherd One moment my little woolly friend. It would seem that in helping them other people you did indeed help the Great Shepherd. You is hereby accorded sheep status and may depart to the right.

Lamb   I'm a sheep?

Shepherd You is indeed a sheep.

Lamb   And I can go to the green pastures and still waters?

Shepherd You can.

Lamb   You know these green pastures?

Shepherd Yes.

Lamb   It is just grass isn't it?

Shepherd Grass and herbs and wild flowers. Why?

Lamb   It's just that I get a bit nervous around mint.

END

A MOTHER'S WORRY

Characters

Ruth

Margaret, the mother of Nicodemus

Bible Background

Jesus and Nicodemus - being born again.   John 3.1-12

A room. Ruth is knitting as Margaret enters.

Margaret   Have you seen him?

Ruth   Who?

Margaret   Nicodemus.

Ruth   Nicodemus? No. Why, is he missing?

Margaret   He's been wandering around in a daze since last night.

Ruth   What happened last night?

Margaret   He went to see that Rabbi.

Ruth   Which one?

Margaret   That Jesus, from Nazareth.

Ruth   What's wrong with that? I'd have thought you'd be delighted that your son seeks out the company of rabbis.

Margaret   Well normally I would be; but he came home in such a state last night. He was muttering all sorts of absurd things.

Ruth   Like what?

Margaret   Like that he must be born again.

Ruth   Born again!

Margaret   I told him that it was bad enough the first time around and that I wasn't going through it all again. The nausea, the dizziness, the fainting ... his father couldn't stand it.

9

	It wasn't that much fun for me either.

Ruth Are you sure he said he had to be born again? Perhaps he was saying he was bored again. Some of these holy men can be very dull.

Margaret Not this Jesus. He does miraculous signs, tells stories, argues with the pharisees. You wouldn't be bored listening to him.

Ruth Well it doesn't stop him talking nonsense. Being born again! Who ever heard of such a thing. What if everyone went around being born again? Think of the mess.

Margaret It was bad enough when he was only this big. *(She holds her hands out to indicate the size of a baby.)* He must be nearly six foot now.

Ruth It would be physically impossible. Besides he's got a beard. It would tickle.

Margaret I hadn't thought of that.

Ruth Why does this Jesus think your Nicodemus needs to be born again?

Margaret Heaven knows.

Ruth Typical rabbi, always bringing heaven into it.

Margaret No, I mean I don't know why Nicodemus needs to be born again. He's a good man, a devout man. And he's clever. He knows all about the law and the holy scriptures. If anyone is going to please God it's going to be him.

Ruth Exactly. And besides, he'd end up like a helpless baby if he was born again. He'd be no use to anyone.

Margaret You can see why I'm concerned. Will you keep an eye on him? He only met Jesus last night and he's already contemplating doing impossible things

Ruth Think what might happen if they met again.

Margaret	Became friends, even.
Ruth	He might go from wanting a new birth to a new life.
Margaret	Let's hope it's just a phase he's going through.
Ruth	I wouldn't worry if I were you. After all, nothing lasts forever.
Margaret	I'm sure you're right. Still, I can't help being concerned.
Ruth	You just want the best for your son. Any parent would. And remember, whatever we think of him, Jesus is somebody's son too.
Margaret	You're right of course. I wonder if we know him?
Ruth	Who?
Margaret	Jesus' father.
Ruth	Oh I doubt that. What kind of father would let his son go around telling people they must be born again?
Margaret	Heaven knows.

END

BAAING UNCERTAINTIES

Characters

Baabara the Sheep
Gary the Sheep

Bible Background

Christmas   Matthew 2.1-12 and Luke 2.1-18

A field

Baab.	Hello, how are you? I'm sorry, I've forgotten your name.
Gary	Gary, Gary the Sheep.
Baab.	I'm Baabara the Sheep.
Gary	Hello.
Baab.	I haven't seen you around much recently.
Gary	I've been busy. How are things with you?
Baab.	Oh quiet. Very quiet. Apart from the angelic hosts.
Gary	Oh yes, those angelic hosts can be a right pain. One minute you're quietly grazing; the next the sky's lit up and angelic hosts are singing and proclaiming all over the place.
Baab.	Dreadful. You'd think they'd have a bit of consideration.
Gary	I nearly choked on a mouthful of clover.
Baab.	What was all that about then?
Gary	Well I had quite a full mouth and you know how tricky clover can be.
Baab.	I meant the angelic hosts.
Gary	Oh right. I'm with you. I don't know. It upset the humans though.
Baab.	You show me something that doesn't. Derek the Wolf

12

	popped by the other day and you should have seen the fuss they made.
Gary	My humans were sat around the fire when the angels popped up and started telling them about a new king who had been born in a stable.
Baab.	I know. They were shocked that a king should be born in a stable.
Gary	Well so was I. The lucky thing. I was born in an open field.
Baab.	That's typical of royalty. They have a privileged birth and they think they're better than the rest of us.
Gary	Did your human go down and visit this new king in his la-di-da stable?
Baab.	Yes. And do you know what he found? He found the royal baby asleep in a manger.
Gary	A manger! What with all that soft straw?
Baab.	Yes. The child will grow up spoiled if they molly-coddle him like that.
Gary	He must have been several hours old by then.
Baab.	I know. I was already putting in a hard days frolicking by the time I was his age.
Gary	They don't know they're born.
Baab.	That's not the worst of it.
Gary	No?
Baab.	This stable, right, it only had some cattle in it lowing.
Gary	Get away. He shared his stable with cattle?
Baab.	That's the truth, I swear.
Gary	Luxury, sheer luxury. All that free body heat.
Baab.	Mind you, there is a down side to having an aristocratic birth. This one attracted a whole lot of unwanted attention.

13

Gary	Oh yes?
Baab.	Three wise men turned up ... on camels.
Gary	Camels. Oh dear.
Baab.	Well you know what they say about camels.
Gary	A horse designed by committee.
Baab.	These wise men brought presents. Gold, Frankincense and Myrrh.
Gary	What did they want to do that for?
Baab.	I expect it's traditional - bringing presents to new born kings .
Gary	I just got a splodge of red dye daubed on my backside so the shepherd knew who I belonged too.
Baab.	Gold, frankincense and myrrh. What is myrrh for anyway?
Gary	I've heard humans anoint dead bodies with it.
Baab.	(Sarcastically) What a charming thing to give to a new born child.
Gary	A bit like giving one of us mint sauce.
	Pause
Baab.	You know this baby king, right?
Gary	Yes.
Baab.	What exactly is he king of then? I mean is he just a king for the humans or is he our king as well?
Gary	If he were our king he'd have to have been born a lamb.
Baab.	I can't see it myself. We sheep have a tough time of it. No proper home, at the mercy of predators, and the best we can hope for is to end up as a sacrifice at the temple. What kind of king is going to choose a life like that?
Gary	Well there's no point bleating on about it.
Baab.	No. I suppose not.
Gary	I'd better be off. I've got heaps to do.

14

Baab.	Oh yes? What are you up to?
Gary	I've got to go and practise leaping over that fence.
Baab.	Why?
Gary	I heard one of the shepherds say that one day I'd make a great woolly jumper.

END

CRY WOLF!

Characters

Narrator 1
Narrator 2
Wolf
Lamb

Bible Background

Parable of the lost sheep.   Luke 15.1-7

A field

Narr.1	Once upon a time.
Narr.2	In a land far away.
Narr.1	There lived a flock of sheep.
Narr.2	And a big bad wolf.
Wolf	Well hello! And what have we got here?
Lamb	I'm a lamb and my name is Meadow.
Wolf	Meadow the Lamb, hey? What a lovely name. Most of the Lambs I've known have been called Rackov, or Leggov, or even Spring Fresh New Zealand.
Lamb	Please sir, will you tell me your name?
Wolf	You may call me Mr Lupine. And where are you travelling to so late in the evening Miss Meadow?
Lamb	I'm going on an adventure.
Wolf	Why how exciting.
Lamb	I'm going to the big city to seek my fortune.
Wolf	Really? Then this is indeed a propitious meeting for I am something of an expert when it comes to the big city. Perhaps I may be of some assistance.

Lamb	Thank you very much kind sir, but my mummy told me never to talk to strangers so I'd best be going on alone.
Wolf	But where is your dear mother?
Lamb	She's back in the field with the rest of the flock.
Wolf	And she doesn't mind you being out alone?
Lamb	I've run away from home.
Wolf	Have you indeed?
Lamb	I've decided I don't need the rest of the flock bossing me about and eating all the best grass. I'm going to make my own way in the world.
Wolf	Good for you. Have you eaten?
Lamb	No.
Wolf	Would you like to be? I mean, me neither.
Lamb	Do you eat grass?
Wolf	Of course, I'm strictly vegetarian. Why don't you come back to my house for supper?
Lamb	No thank you.
Wolf	I insist.
Lamb	My mummy wouldn't like it and nor would the Shepherd.
Wolf	*(Looking about anxiously)* Shepherd? What shepherd?
Lamb	He looks out over my flock and makes sure we are led to green pastures and have enough to drink.
Wolf	But I expect he's very cruel. Very strict.
Lamb	No, he's very kind. And he protects us from danger.
Wolf	Oh yes? What kinds of danger?
Lamb	From getting lost or trapped or being eaten by wolves.
Wolf	Really? But I suppose he's back watching your flock now.
Lamb	Yes, he's a long way away. And the flock will be gathered together to tell stories about the legendary Bo Peep incident, and to wonder about the greatest mysteries of all time - like, whatever happened to the little boy who

17

	lived down the lane.
Wolf	It sounds very cosy.
Lamb	About now they'll be discussing Mary and why she took one of us to school with her.
Wolf	As a snack for playtime perhaps?
Lamb	And then they'll all snuggle down for the night, keeping each other warm and comfortable.
Wolf	I have a little room that will keep you warm. I call it my aga.
Lamb	Gosh I miss them all.
Wolf	But not for much longer.
Lamb	Oh I know they used to baa and bleat on and on about silly little things like whether sheep should be dipped as adults or as lambs. And whether it was okay for ewes to attend gatherings when they'd been shorn.
Wolf	How petty. You don't need them.
Lamb	But I need something.
Wolf	How about seasoning.
Lamb	I wish I knew the way home.
Wolf	Home? Why do you want to go home? They've forgotten all about you by now. You've been abandoned. Come with me and see the real world. It'll consume you.
Lamb	Do you really think I've been forgotten?
Wolf	I'd bet my entire collection of fresh mint on it.
Lamb	Oh. I don't suppose your kind offer to have me for dinner is still open?
Wolf	I can't think of anything nicer. Come on.

They start to exit

| Lamb | Look! *(Pointing off stage)* It's the shepherd. He's come all this way looking for me. Mr Shepherd! Mr Shepherd! |

Over here. I want you meet a friend of mine. *(Turns to find the wolf exiting rapidly in the opposite direction)* That's strange!

The lamb skips off happily with the Shepherd

Wolf   Curses! Foiled again. Now I'll have to see what I've got in the freezer. Oh yes, I think there's still some little boy who lived down the lane left.

END

EDEN'S TURNING

Characters

Lion

Tiger

Bible Background

The Fall of humankind. Genesis 2.4 - 3.24

The Garden of Eden - with token pot plant?

Lion	Once upon a time, in the Garden of Eden ...
Tiger	... Everything was perfect and every creature ...
Lion	... Lived in harmony one with another.
Tiger	Presumably every creature was a vegetarian.
Lion	Hello.
Tiger	Hello.
Lion	Lovely day.
Tiger	Wonderful.
Lion	Lovely garden.
Tiger	Beautiful.
Lion	Paradise in fact.
Tiger	Paradise indeed.
Lion	Are you enjoying eating that grass?
Tiger	Is that what it's called?
Lion	Apparently. I'm Lion, pleased to meet you.
Tiger	Hi, I'm ... I'm sorry I've forgotten my name. I've only had it a few days and ...
Lion	Oh I know! That happened to me just the other day. Someone was shouting "Oy Lion, stop playing with that ball of wool." It was an age before I realised they were

	shouting at me.
Tiger	Is the sheep all right now?
Lion	Much better. I was so embarrassed.
Tiger	Well it takes time to get used to new things. I mean, what's with all this naming? Who decided you were going to be called Lion?
Lion	I rather fancied Trevor myself.
Tiger	That funny pink creature balancing on two legs gave me my name ... Oh I wish I could remember what it was.
Lion	Adam.
Tiger	No.
Lion	No, Adam was the one dishing out the names.
Tiger	Why was that?
Lion	He's a friend of the Creator. He's been put in charge of names.
Tiger	Really? Tough job. Lots of responsibility that.
Lion	I'll say. Would you have fancied finding a name for those things with funny noses and flappy things.
Tiger	What birds?
Lion	Elephants.
Tiger	This Adam who has been put in charge.
Lion	Yes.
Tiger	I saw him hiding in those bushes earlier. He was with the other two legged pink thing.
Lion	The Flamingo?
Tiger	No, Eve, the woman.
Lion	Oh, her. Who were they hiding from?
Tiger	The Creator I think. From what I could see things looked distinctly chilly between them.
Lion	Well they don't have much fur to speak of.
Tiger	They were having a row.

21

Lion	I thought they were all buddy-buddy.
Tiger	Not from what I could see.
Lion	So there's trouble in paradise, is there?
Tiger	Well something's happened. You can sense it.
Lion	I wonder if it's got anything to do with that fruit tree.
Tiger	Why do you say that?
Lion	It's just that I saw the snake talking to the woman over there. He was giving her an apple.
Tiger	No harm in that.
Lion	I suppose not. It's just that it looked a bit under-hand; you know, sneaky.
Tiger	I've never liked that snake. It's the way he can unhinge his jaw. He says it's so he can eat melons whole but I've seen the way he looks at the rabbit.
Lion	Well we've all been tempted.
Tiger	I don't know what you are talking about, I love grass.
Lion	Of course you do. But haven't you ever looked at a herd of antelopes and just wondered?
Tiger	Well ...
Lion	I can't get the idea out of my head. Ever since I saw the woman take a bite from that apple.
Tiger	The pigs came by with their family of five piglets.
Lion	Six, they had six piglets ... Oh you didn't.
Tiger	I'm so ashamed.
Lion	I don't know what's going on. One minute my mouth was watering at the thought of some fresh mown hay, the next I was drooling over that thing with the hump.
Tiger	What, the camel?
Lion	No, Eve, she was in a right stroppy mood. She was moaning on to Adam that she had no clothes.
Tiger	What did Adam say?

22

Lion	Nothing, he just looked bored hanging around bushes while she tried on different fig leaves. She kept saying the snake had tricked her and asking did her bum look big in this.
Tiger	Personally I think it's time to quit this garden. It used to be wonderful but something's gone wrong.
Lion	I think you're right. Paradise has been lost. Things will never be the same again.
Tiger	Where will you go?
Lion	To the top of the food chain I think.
Tiger	No, where will you live? I fancy India myself.
Lion	I'll head for Africa.
Tiger	What do you think Adam and Eve will do?
Lion	Try and sort out the mess they are in I should think.
Tiger	They'll need help. They're not very bright you know.
Lion	I wouldn't worry. The Creator seems very fond of them. He'll find a way to fix things.
Tiger	I'll be off then. It's been nice meeting you Lion.
Lion	It's been nice meeting you ... er.
Tiger	Tiger! There, I knew it would come to me.
Lion	It's been nice meeting you Tiger. I'll see you around. I'm off for a bite to eat, a snack ... What do you call those things that are hard on the outside but are all soft on the inside?
Tiger	Walnuts?
Lion	Armadillos. Bye. *They exit.*

END

INVITING TROUBLE

Characters

Narrator 1
Narrator 2
Polly
Julian
John
Karen
Master

Bible Background

Parable of the Great Supper. Luke 14.12-24

Narr.1	Once upon a time.
Narr.2	A great man decided to hold a great banquet.
Narr.1	He sent out handwritten invitations on embossed card to all the important people in the town.
Narr.2	And he set his staff to preparing for the great day.
Narr.1	The silver was polished.
Narr.2	The table was laid.
Narr.1	The menu was chosen.
Narr.2	And the napkins were folded
Master	Go
Narr.1	Said the great man.
Master	And tell everyone the banquet is starting.
Narr.2	The servants banged the dinner gong.
Narr.1	They stood ready to take coats and put them on the bed in the spare room,
Narr.2	They waited to hand round glasses of Harvey's Bristol Cream.

Narr.1	And they waited.
Narr.2	And they waited.
Narr.1	And they peered out of the window because they thought they heard someone arriving.
Narr.2	And they checked the date on the calendar.
Narr.1	And they checked the date on the invitations.
Narr.2	And they started to say unto each other.
Karen	I expect the traffic is bad.
Polly	People always arrive a bit late. You know, to let things get going.
John	Perhaps we'd better turn the oven down.
Narr.1	At last one of the servants said.
Julian	I think I'll just pop around the corner and find out what's happened.
Narr.2	So he nipped along the road to see if everything was all right.

Julian knocks on a door. Polly answers it.

Polly	Oh it's tonight is it? I'm so sorry, it completely slipped my mind. I've just bought a new car and we're about to give it a test drive.
Narr.1	So the servant whizzed over to the next house.

Julian knocks on a door. Karen answers it.

Karen	Oh my darling! I'm so sorry. We've just bought a new cottage in the country and we've arranged to go there for the weekend. You've only just caught us in. We were about to leave.
Narr.2	The servant popped across the street to the next guest.

Julian knocks on a door. John answers it.

John	Look you've caught me at a bad time, really. I've just got married and we're having a bit of a domestic.

John ducks as Karen throws an object at the back of John's head. Julian catches it and hands it to John.

John	Thank you. I'm just coming my darling.
Narr.1	And so it went on. Guest after guest made their excuses.
Narr.2	The servant returned to his master and explained the embarrassing fact that no one was coming to the banquet.
Narr.1	The master was deeply hurt. The banquet had cost him a great deal and much effort had gone into its preparation.
Narr.2	So the master instructed his servants to go out into the town and invite anyone they met to come along to the feast.
Polly	What anyone?
Master	Anyone.
John	What even the people with door bells that play "Yankee Doodle Dandy?"
Julian	Or the ones who put their Christmas decorations up in October?
Polly	Or the ones with "Oh no, not you again!" welcome mats.
Master	Anyone. Everyone.
John	But Master, some of these people aren't very ...
Polly	They might not know how to behave properly.
John	They might use the wrong knife when the entree is served.
Polly	They might be ... well ...
Julian	Sire, these people may be embarrassing.
Narr.1	But the Master said.
Master	This is my banquet, my party, I'll invite who I like. You are my servants, go and do as I say.
Narr.2	So the servants got together and said to each other.

Julian	Our master wishes each of us to invite every one we meet to his banquet. What are we going to do?
Karen	He has given us a command, we'll have to obey.
Narr.1	But because the servants were a bit embarrassed, and a bit afraid, of going up to people and inviting them to a feast; they weren't always very good at it.
John	*(In a very stilted manner)* Here, friend, let me give you this to read.
Julian	*(Reading)* Come ye to a feast or burn ye in hell.
Karen	My name is ... er ... Karen, and ... er ... I'd just like to just tell you about ... er ... this feast which I ... er ... just know about.
Narr.2	But slowly the servants got better at telling the people they met in the town about the great feast to which all were invited.
Narr.1	Some of them hired great halls and invited people to hear about the banquet that had been prepared for them.
John	*(In the style of an American Evangelist)* Brothers and sisters, I tell you the truth when I say the table is laden with good things, wholesome things The master invites you to sit down at that table and eat. Consume the vol-a-vent of his generosity, and cover yourselves with the serviettes of his altruism. Eat, ingest and devour!
Narr.2	Other servants found they could tell people about the feast better on a one to one basis.
Karen	*(To Julian)* You look hungry. I know where there's plenty for you to eat.
Narr.1	They began to write songs and to sing about the banquet.

All	*Singing to the Tune of 'All things Bright and Beautiful'*

All food fresh and edible
All veggies great and small
Cakes to make your tummies full
The Master serves them all.

He serves the sherry trifle
The burgers and the fries
The ice cream's rum 'n' raisin
There's steak and kidney pies

All food tastes delectable
All dishes will be served
All wines tasting wonderful
Your place has been reserved.

Narr.2	And so the news spread across the town that a meal was ready to be eaten.
Narr.1	So all who were hungry could be fed.
Narr.2	And all who were thirsty could quench their thirsts.
Narr.1	No one who was invited was turned away.
Narr.2	All that was needed were servants prepared to invite guests on behalf of the master.
Narr.1	To the greatest party of all time.
Polly	Please take your places at the table.
Julian	The feast is ready to begin.

END

GUARD DUTY

Characters

Two guards

Bible Background

Easter. Roman guards and the empty tomb.
Matthew 27.57 - 28.7, 11-15

Two guards stand outside a garden tomb early one Sunday morning.

A   Who did you say we were supposed to be guarding?

B   That Jesus, from Nazareth.

They look in the tomb.

A   He's definitely gone.

B   I can see that.

A   Dead bodies don't usually get up and leave do they?

B   Not usually, no.

A   He really was dead wasn't he? I mean, they couldn't have made a mistake, could they?

B   They hung him on a blooming big wooden cross with nails here, here and here. *(Indicates points on wrists and feet of Guard A)* Once on the cross he either stood in agony on this nail here *(Indicates place where nail would pierce feet)* so he could breathe, or he hung from these nails here and here *(Indicates wrists)* and suffocated. Besides, one of the lads shoved a spear in his side, here.

A   So he was definitely dead then.

B   Dead! Of course he was dead! Why do you think they buried him?

29

A	But he's gone
B	Well he can't have gone far.
A	He shouldn't have gone anywhere.
B	Well he has.
A	What are you going to tell the sergeant?
B	I ... What do you mean, what am I going to tell the sergeant?
A	You're in charge.
B	Oh no I'm not.
A	You are!
B	Not!
A	Are!
B	Not!
A	Are!
B	Not!
A	Well someone's got to tell him something.
B	And what exactly do you propose we tell him? Hi Sarge, you know that very dead body you left us guarding? Well it's gone and given us the slip.
A	He's not going to be very pleased, is he?
B	No he's not. If we're really lucky he'll only feed us to the lions.
A	I know! We'll tell him some people came and stole the body. His friends or followers or someone.
B	Brilliant! Hi Sarge, we've just been overpowered by a group of religious fanatics. Yes Sarge, we were armed. No Sarge, we haven't got any captives or witnesses. Yes Sarge, I'm very fond of cats.
A	Then there's only one last thing we can try.
B	Anything.
A	We'll have to distract people from the truth.

B	What, that we've mislaid the body of a prominent religious figure?
A	Yes.
B	That the evidence would seem to indicate that he just got up and left.
A	Yes.
B	That if he is raised from the dead then it's just about the most important event in the history of everything?
A	Yes.
B	It's going to have to be one heck of a distraction.
A	I don't suppose you'd consider dressing up as a six-foot rabbit and handing out chocolate eggs to small children.
B	Do you think that would work?
A	Consider the alternative.
B	What alternative?
A	Centurions - nine out of ten cats prefer them.

END

INN TROUBLE

Characters

Jacob, a traveller
Ruth, the innkeeper's wife.

Bible Background

Parable of the Good Samaritan. Luke 10.25-37

A room in an inn.
Enter Jacob. He is using a walking stick and his arm is in a sling.
Enter Ruth, the innkeeper's wife.

Ruth   You're up then?

Jacob   Yes. Where am I?

Ruth   You're at the Jericho Road Hotel, Inn and Country Club.
Are you feeling any better? This isn't a hospital, you
know.

Jacob   I'm feeling a bit better. My head still aches. I felt I needed
a little fresh air.

Ruth   Are you saying that the room we've put you in is stuffy?

Jacob   No, no. It's a lovely room.

Ruth   I'm glad you think so, it's one of our best. That Samaritan
gentleman who brought you here insisted we look after
you.

Jacob   And you have. This is a lovely inn, just lovely, it's really
... lovely.

Ruth   We run a high class establishment here.

Jacob   I can see that. I particularly appreciate the way you fold
the end of the toilet paper into a neat triangle. Er ... How
long have I been here for?

Ruth	Don't you remember?
Jacob	Not really. Things are a bit hazy.
Ruth	Then it's nearly two weeks that you've been here.
Jacob	Two weeks?
Ruth	Two weeks, staying in one of our best, most expensive, rooms.
Jacob	And you say a Samaritan brought me here.
Ruth	Yes. You were in a right state. You bled all over the foyer.
Jacob	I'm sorry. Um ... Did this Samaritan say what had happened to me?
Ruth	You were mugged.
Jacob	By whom?
Ruth	Muggers. They beat you to a pulp. I've never seen so much blood. It's amazing you're alive really.
Jacob	I dimly remember somebody trying to choke me with some foul tasting liquid.
Ruth	Do you mind. My mother gave me that chicken soup recipe.
Jacob	And I remember a long series of repeated bumps followed by a burning sensation.
Ruth	We had to get you up the stairs somehow. And it's a long corridor to drag someone along. The state you were in I'm surprised you noticed a few extra carpet burns.
Jacob	And there was a tremendous bang on the head.
Ruth	You know the shelf above your bed?
Jacob	What shelf?
Ruth	Exactly. But don't worry, we've put the damage on your bill.
Jacob	How much is my bill?
Ruth	We haven't worked it out precisely. But my Ernie reckons it could be a record amount. Especially with the single

	room supplement.
Jacob	But I haven't got any money. I was robbed, remember?
Ruth	Then it's a good job your friend the Samaritan is footing the bill for you.
Jacob	But I haven't got any Samaritan friends.
Ruth	This one said he was a neighbour of yours.
Jacob	A neighbour?
Ruth	That's what he said. You're lucky to have such caring neighbours. Others aren't so lucky. Just before you were brought in here we had a priest and a Levite staying. They both said they'd seen some poor old soul lying in the road bleeding. They had to cross the road to avoid the blood.
Jacob	You mean two people, a priest and a ...
Ruth	Levite, yes.
Jacob	Walked by on the other side of the road while I lay bleeding?
Ruth	Oh no, it couldn't have been you. The person they saw was just a nobody.
Jacob	But what made me different?
Ruth	You've got a friend. That makes all the difference. He bandaged you up, carried you here on his own donkey, and paid for your room and board. You're really lucky. You've got someone who cares about you. Someone prepared to risk getting involved. We should all have friends like yours.
Jacob	Yes. I wonder who he was. I think I'm going back to my room to lie down. I still feel a bit woozy.
Ruth	Well you have been through a terrible ordeal. It takes a while to get over being mugged and robbed. Oh, and poisoned.

34

Jacob	Poisoned?
Ruth	I'm sorry, but you have to be so careful when you reheat chicken soup.

END

THE BURNING ISSUE

Characters

Beverley
Aaron (off-stage for the whole sketch)

Bible Background

Moses and Aaron take on the Egyptians. Exodus 3 and 4

The offices of the Egyptian Brickworks Company. In this monologue Aaron is busy measuring bricks offstage. Beverley, his secretary, answers the phone.

Beverley   Hello, The Egyptian Brickwork Company, Mr Aaron's office. My name is Beverly, how may I help you? ... I'm afraid Mr Aaron is busy just at the moment. May I take a message? Who shall I say was calling?
(She calls to Aaron)
Mr Aaron, there's a gentleman here who says he's your brother. I didn't know you had a brother.
(To Moses)
Can I take your name please? Moses. Ah ha. What, like the basket? ... Oh, that was you was it. Lovely.
(She calls to Aaron)
He says his name is Moses. Like the basket.
(To Moses)
He's ever so busy Mr Moses. The Egyptians are working him like a ... well, like a slave. It's not fair, it really isn't. Someone ought to do something about it.
Where are you calling from? Exile. You had to go into exile after the unfortunate incident with the Egyptian.

What was unfortunate about it? You killed him. Yes, I can see how that would be considered unfortunate. What message would you like to give Mr Aaron? You've been speaking to a ... a what? I thought you said a bush. Oh you did.

(She calls to Aaron)

Your brother has been talking to a shrubbery. *(She listens)* I'll ask.

(To Moses)

Mr Aaron would like to know what kind of shrub you have been conversing with ... I see.

(She calls to Aaron)

He says it was difficult to tell what with it being on fire. *(She listens)* I'll ask.

(To Moses)

Did you set it on fire yourself? *(She holds the receiver away from her ear as if someone were shouting down it.)* I was only asking. You've already admitted to murder. You could easily be an arsonist for all I know ... No, no, I'm sorry. I certainly don't think you're the kind of man who goes around igniting his environment. No, I don't think you're mad. What you get up to in the privacy of your own desert is entirely up to you. I'll just write down your message. ... Oh, the message is not exactly from you ... It's from the bush. Lovely.

(She calls to Aaron)

He says the burning bush spoke to him. *(She listens)* I'll ask.

(To Moses)

Does this bush have a name? ... I AM WHO I AM. Would that be all in block capitals? Yes, I should think so. What

37

did the bush say? ... "Take off your sandals." It sounds very house-proud for a bit of greenery. It had just vacuumed had it? Oh I see. "Take off your sandals for the place you are standing is holy ground. I am the God of your father, the God of Abraham, the God of Isaac and the God of Jacob." Coo!

(She calls to Aaron)

Don't worry, he hasn't gone doo-lally, it turns out the bush was God. Undercover, so to speak ... I'll ask.

(To Moses)

Your brother wants to know what God was doing hanging about in the wilderness disguised as a bush waiting to talk to you.

(She listens) I see.

(She calls to Aaron)

He wanted to give him a special mission.

(To Moses)

What like "this bush will self-destruct in five seconds" kind of thing? Surely the bush should have burst into flames after it gave you the message ... Right, I'm listening. You have to go to Pharaoh and demand that he set God's people free. This is a suicide mission is it?

(She calls to Aaron)

He wants to go to Pharaoh and demand that our people go free. Isn't that nice.

(She listens)

(To Moses)

Your brother says you do what you like so long as you leave him out of it.

(She listens)

(She calls to Aaron)

He says God wants you to help him. He says you've got such a lovely speaking voice God has decided you're to be your brother's spokesman. The first thing you've got to do is help him to get the Israelites to listen to God's plan. Isn't that lovely?

(To Moses)

I may have to call you back Mr Moses. Your brother's gone a funny colour. *(She listens)* Right, I'll tell him you'll meet him en route. It was lovely talking to you. I'm a big fan of your baskets. Good luck with your mission. Bye bye.

(She puts down the phone)

Oh, wasn't that nice! It's so important for families to keep in touch.

(She starts to exit)

I'll just get you a map. I think Exile is somewhere near the coast.

END

TOMB TO LET

Characters

Agent
Buyer

Bible Background

Easter. The empty tomb.   Matthew 27.57-60

An estate agent is waiting to show a prospective buyer around a property.
Enter the buyer.

Agent   Welcome, welcome. I'm Nick Snyde of Snyde, Oyle and
Smarm, Estate Agents. We're acting on behalf Mr and
Mrs Arimathea.

Buyer   Hello.

Agent   Let me show you around. As you can see the property is
detached and pleasantly situated in this garden of peace
... Peaceful garden I mean.

Buyer   It doesn't look very big.

Agent   Bijou. It's very bijou.

Buyer   It doesn't seem to have a front door.

Agent   Yes it does.

Buyer   Where?

Agent   Here.

Buyer   But that's just a large rock.

Agent   Well yes. But as a door it does have many special
features.

Buyer   Such as?

Agent   It'll never blow shut in the wind. In addition, you'll never
lose your keys.

40

Buyer	But what about security?
Agent	Er ... it has a dead bolt. Shall we go in.

The agent and buyer stoop very low as if going through a very small door. Once 'inside' they stand as if in a very small room with a low ceiling.

Buyer	It's a bit cramped.
Agent	We prefer to think of it as cosy. Nice and easy to keep warm.
Buyer	Where's the bedroom?
Agent	It's a studio flat. May I draw your attention to the multi-purpose furnishing unit. It's a combination work surface, dining table, and bed.
Buyer	It looks a bit like a stone ledge.
Agent	Which is in keeping with the rest of the decor.
Buyer	I'm sorry, but it doesn't feel very ... lived in.
Agent	Yes ... well there is a good reason for that.
Buyer	Did the previous occupier live here long?
Agent	Live? No. He was just a temporary tenant as it turned out.
Buyer	How long was he here for?
Agent	Three days.
Buyer	Didn't he like it?
Agent	Let's just say it didn't suit his change of circumstances.
Buyer	Oh? What were they?
Agent	I think it's fair to say they were life changing.
Buyer	I'd like to know why he decided to move out so quickly. I mean, did he have trouble with the neighbours?
Agent	Hardly. They're very quiet.
Buyer	Even so, would it be possible to talk to him?
Agent	That might be difficult.
Buyer	Why? He must have left a forwarding address.

41

Agent	I'm afraid he didn't.
Buyer	But he can't have vanished off the face of the earth. Someone must have seen him.
Agent	I believe quite a number of people have seen him, yes.
Buyer	So it must be possible to talk to him. After all, it's not as if he's dead, is it?
Agent	Not anymore, no.
Buyer	I'm afraid I really don't understand.
Agent	Funny. I met a couple of soldiers the other day who were saying exactly the same thing.
Buyer	Look, can I meet him or not?
Agent	You'll need to talk to some of his friends.
Buyer	And where can I find them?
Agent	They seem to be all over the place.
Buyer	Oh this is ridiculous! Look, I'm sorry to have wasted your time, but I don't think this is the kind of place I'm looking for. It feels a bit cold somehow, a bit empty.
Agent	That's fine Madam. There are plenty of other people interested in this property. In fact I have a gentleman coming to view in just a little while. He's looking for somewhere to get away from it all, he says. Somewhere to bring back memories. He says this is just the kind of place he's looking for.
Buyer	Good. I hope he's very happy here. Goodbye.
Agent	Goodbye Madam. Ah, here is my next appointment. Good afternoon, how are you Mr Lazarus?

END

WORKERS' RIGHTS

Characters

Shop steward
Worker

Bible Background

Parable of the Good Employer.   Matthew 20.1-16

A Committee room

Shop S. Brothers! Sisters! Calm yourselves. Thank you. I know we are all upset but nothing will be achieved if we don't behave with a little decorum. I'm calling this meeting to order.

Worker Order! Order! Order!

Shop S. Thank you sister.

Worker Order! Order!

Shop S. Yes, thank you sister.

Worker Order!

Shop S. Sister!

Worker Ord ...

Shop S. Shut up!

Worker Sorry.

Shop S. Brothers and Sister, I know feelings are running high. I'm told that never in the history of the National Union of Vineworkers has there been such a challenge to our working practices.

Worker It's outrageous.

Shop S. Yes it is outrageous.

Worker It's scandalous!

Shop S.	Yes it is scandalous.
Worker	It's ...
Shop S.	It's time you shut up and sat down before I pass a motion that you be taken outside, painted bright red and dumped in the field that has a big 'Beware of the bull' sign nailed to the gate.
Worker	Sorry. It's just that I feel affronted.
Shop S.	You'll feel a great big pair of horns if you don't keep quiet.
Worker	I'll sit here then shall I?
Shop S.	Yes.
Worker	Fine.
Shop S.	I've convened this meeting to discuss the incident that happened yesterday at the vineyard. This is just another example of managements attempts to exploit the work force and increase profits at the expense of established working practices.
Worker	Yes.
Shop S.	A fair day's work for a fair day's pay.
Worker	Yes.
Shop S.	That principle is enshrined in our constitution. And what is a fair day's wage?
Worker	I know!
Shop S.	That was a rhetorical question.
Worker	Well I still know the answer.
Shop S.	A fair day's wage is one denarius.
Worker	I knew that.
Shop S.	But what did the vineyard owner pay for a fair day's work?
Worker	One denarius.
Shop S.	He paid ... what?
Worker	One denarius.

44

Shop S.	But you said he wasn't paying a fair wage.
Worker	He wasn't.
Shop S.	One denarius is a perfectly fair wage. I negotiated the rate myself.
Worker	But he's not paying one denarius for a fair day's work. He's paying one denarius for an unfair day's work.
Shop S.	You mean he's making you work more than twelve hours for one denarius?
Worker	No, he's making us work less. At least he's making some of us work less. Some of us only had to work for nine hours for one denarius.
Shop S.	Nine hours?
Worker	And some of us only had to work for six hours for one denarius.
Shop S.	Six?
Worker	And some only worked for three hours.
Shop S.	Three?
Worker	And I personally only had to work for one hour, but I was still paid one whole denarius.
Shop S.	Let me understand this; you are complaining because you were paid a whole denarius for just one hours work?
Worker	Absolutely! Well no, not really. Actually one denarius per hour seems a very reasonable rate of pay.
Shop S.	Yes it does. So what exactly is our perfectly legitimate grievance with the management? Why have we bought wine production to a halt across the whole region? For what purpose has this industrial action been called? Why are we on strike? Because you have been paid twelve times the normal rate of pay!
Worker	But what about those workers who worked all day for the same amount of money? Surely they should receive

	more money for working more hours. That's only fair.
Shop S.	They agreed to work for one denarius. One denarius for twelve hours work. We negotiated that wage. Everyone agreed it was fair. You agreed it was fair!
Worker	So what's your point.
Shop S.	How can we call a national vineworkers strike because the management is being unreasonably generous? What do you suggest our slogan is? Less pay - More Work!?
Worker	But it doesn't seem right. People who do fewer hours work should be paid less than those who do a whole days work. That's common sense that is.
Shop S.	It may be common sense to you or to me, but it evidently isn't to the vineyard owner. If he wants to pay a flat rate for however long you work then that is his right. It's his money after all. I cannot call a strike over this issue.
Worker	But think of the consequences if we don't take a stand.
Shop S.	What consequences? The vineyard owner getting the grapes harvested on time? Everyone having enough money for food? Everyone being able to afford their union subscription?
Worker	But supposing all the bosses start treating their work forces fairly, paying them generously, and refusing to exploit casual labourers. We wouldn't need a union then. *(Pause)*
Shop S.	Everybody out!
Both	*(Chanting)* What do we want? Less Pay! When do we want it? Now!

END

46

MAKING WAVES

Characters

Thaddeus

Lydia

Bible Background

Jesus walks on water and calms a storm. Matthew 6.45-52

*Thaddeus and Lydia are aboard a small boat, at night, in the middle of the
sea of Galilee. The weather is inclement.*
Six chairs sideways on to the congregation representing the boat.
*Thaddeus and Lydia each sit astride one chair.   They can rock from side to
side. Background sounds of a rough sea could be used.*

Thaddeus Bail!

Lydia I'm bailing!

Thaddeus Well bail harder. We're going to sink at this rate.

Lydia Well if we do, it'll all be your fault.

Thaddeus Somehow I knew that it would be.

Lydia Can't we get back to the shore?

Thaddeus I don't even know in which direction the shore is
anymore. I think I'm going to be sick again.

Lydia Well try and do it over the side this time.

Thaddeus Keep bailing. Do you want us to sink?

Lydia Let's not walk all the way around the lake, you said.
Let's hire a boat and sail across, you said. It'll be a
pleasure, you said. Didn't you check the weather
forecast?

Thaddeus Listen, when we set out it was a beautiful sunny day. I
didn't hear you complaining then.

47

Lydia   That was before I knew I was going to drown in the middle of the sea of Galilee, at night, in a storm. Next time you want me to get in a boat with you, not that there is going to be a next time, I'm going to check that your name really is Thaddeus and not Jonah.

Thaddeus You were the one who wanted a day out. It wasn't my idea to go traipsing off into the wilderness to hear that teacher Jesus preach. It'll be fun, you said. The whole exercise has been a disaster from beginning to end.

Lydia   I've said I'm sorry for forgetting the picnic, but I wasn't the only one.

Thaddeus That's true. Over five thousand people and not a caterer in sight. It looked for a while as if no one was going to be able to hear Jesus preach because of the noise of people's stomachs rumbling. All I can say is that it's a jolly good thing that someone remembered to bring all that bread and those fish.

Lydia   If you hadn't eaten so much you wouldn't have minded walking home.

Thaddeus I thought hiring a boat would make a nice change. How was I to know that the weather was going to be so awful this evening? Look, we're not the only ones caught out here. See?

Lydia   Where? I can't see anything.

Thaddeus Over there. It's another boat. Ahoy!

Lydia   I can see it. It's the boat those friends of Jesus took after the meeting. You know, to get away from the crowds. They must be going to Gennesaret too.

Thaddeus It looks as if they are in as much trouble as us. Ahoy!

Lydia   Help! It's no good, they can't hear us above the noise of the wind.

Thaddeus I doubt if they could help us anyway. They look as lost as we are.

Lydia Er ... Thaddeus? How deep is this lake?

Thaddeus Very, very deep, Lydia. Why?

Lydia Well, it's just that someone appears to be taking a stroll across it.

Thaddeus Don't be silly, dear. No-one's going to go out for a stroll in weather like this.

Lydia It's probably someone in a hurry to get home. This is probably a short cut.

Thaddeus What are you talking about? We're miles from the shore. Good grief, there is someone walking on the water.

Lydia Isn't that Jesus?

Thaddeus What's he doing out here?

Lydia He's going over to the other boat. Look, someone's getting out of it and walking towards him. Perhaps he's going to ask for directions.

Thaddeus We don't need directions out here, we need a miracle.

Lydia I think it's that Peter. You know, the one we saw trying to persuade that small boy to give up his fish supper. Oh look, he appears to be getting shorter.

Thaddeus He's not getting shorter, dear, he's sinking.

Lydia Do something, Thaddeus.

Thaddeus Do what?

Lydia Dive in and save him. He's going to drown. You've got to save him.

Thaddeus But I can't swim.

Lydia All you have to do is flap your legs and move your arms about. I'm sure you'll get the hang of it. Quickly, the poor man is getting wet.

Thaddeus Don't look at me! I can't do anything about it. I'm not the

49

one who encouraged him to go paddling.

Lydia It's all right. Jesus is reaching out to him. Peter's being rescued by Jesus. Now they're both getting into the boat.

Thaddeus Oh I am glad. Jesus has rescued Peter, whoopee! We are about to drown in the middle of a lake and Jesus has to spend his time fishing for fishermen who are too stupid to stay on the inside of their boat. What about us?

Lydia Thaddeus.

Thaddeus We're going to die. My life is flashing before me.

Lydia Thaddeus.

Thaddeus Have you got a straw on you?

Lydia A straw? Why?

Thaddeus I want to clutch at it.

Lydia Thaddeus, the wind has dropped. The sea is calming.

Thaddeus Don't interrupt me, I'm preparing to meet my maker.

Lydia Open your eyes. I think you will find him in that boat over there.

Thaddeus I don't believe it.

Lydia But you saw him walking on the water. You saw him calm the storm.

Thaddeus I believe that, I'm not stupid.

Lydia Then what don't you believe?

Thaddeus One minute I'm in a boat caught up in a howling wind, the next it's completely calm.

Lydia Isn't that the miracle you wanted? A calm sea. We're saved.

Thaddeus Yes, a calm sea. Not a breath of wind. A miracle. There's just one thing.

Lydia What?

Thaddeus No oars.

Lydia Oh dear. Then there's just one thing for it.

Thaddeus What?

Lydia It's only a few miles. We'll just have to walk.

END

YOU MUST BE BORN AGAIN AGAIN

Characters

Beth

Nicodemus

Bible Background

Being born again.   John 3.1-12

Nicodemus off stage right throws scrolls on to stage as his wife rushes on stage left.

Beth	Nicodemus!
Nic.	*(Off stage right)* Yes, my dear.
Beth	What are you doing, we're going to be late for the synagogue.
Nic.	*(Entering quickly from stage right clutching more scrolls)* I'm just recycling these old scrolls. I thought we could re-use the papyrus.

He puts scrolls onto table and unrolls a few of them, inspecting them.

Beth	But why ?
Nic.	Papyrus doesn't grow on trees, you know. One day the world will run out of reeds.
Beth	Well hurry up. That new Rabbi Jesus is going to speak.
Nic.	Yes dear.
Beth	And why is there a pile of used wine-skins outside the back door?
Nic.	So we can use them again.
Beth	But we could buy some new ones.

Nic.   That's typical of this modern day and age.   Use something once, then throw it away.

As if to illustrate, he tosses a scroll stage left.

Beth   What else do you suggest we do ?

Nic.   I told you, recycle things. *(He retrieves scroll)* At the rate things are going, we're not going to make it to end of the First Century.

Beth   You are cracking up, you know. I thought you were when I saw that note you left pinned to the firewood: "Use this wood carefully - you can only burn it once"

Nic.   Well, what's wrong with that ? It's true !

Beth   The Good Lord gave us this world to do with as we like. Most of the land is taken up with useless forest and jungle. If we started chopping trees down now, it would be two thousand years before we'd have to start worrying.

Nic.   That's exactly my point. It may take a while, but one day people will look around them and wonder where all the forests have gone !

He illustrates by placing some scrolls on their end, then toppling them over.

Beth   Nonsense ! They're as common as Dodo's. Now will you get a move on !

Nic.   Yes dear. *(He abandons the scrolls, his wife helps him to put on his coat)* Do you know what this Jesus will be preaching about?

Beth   According to the synagogue notices the theme is Eternal Life.

Nic.   I like him already. Some one who takes the long term

	view of things.
Beth	I doubt he'll be ranting on about recycling things though.
Nic.	You never know. Does it give a text from which he'll be preaching ?
Beth	No. But there is a title to his sermon.
Nic.	What is it ?
Beth	You Must Be Born Again.
Nic.	*(In triumph)* There you are - if that's not recycling, I don't know what is!

END

NO ROOM AT THE STABLE

Characters

Clive

Hester

Bible Background

Christmas.   Matthew 2.1-12 and Luke 2.1-7

The reception desk of the Bethlehem Inn. Hester, the innkeeper's wife is at the desk.

Enter Clive, a travelling salesman.

Clive   'Evening Madam.

Hester   Good evening, sir. Welcome to the Bethlehem Inn. Do you have a reservation?

Clive   Yes indeedy. Name of Shekel, Clive Shekel. Shekel's the name, sales is my game. That's what I always say.

Hester   Ah yes. Mr Shekel, room 24. I'll arrange to have someone carry your bags.

Clive   Bit busy in town tonight isn't it?

Hester   Very busy sir. It's the census you see. Caesar Augustus has decreed that everyone register in the town that their family comes from originally. It's a good job you booked your room well in advance. I've been turning people away all day. We're packed to the rafters.

Clive   Good for business, hey?

Hester   Excellent sir.

Clive   Well, I'll just pop up to my room for a wash and brush up before supper. Could you get one of your staff to park my donkey in your stable?

Hester	Your donkey, sir?
Clive	My donkey, yes. I'm a travelling salesman, how do you expect me to travel? It's a company mule. You'll find it out there with a fine set of alloy horseshoes and set of fluffy dice hanging from the saddle.
Hester	It's just that our stable is a bit full at the moment.
Clive	That's not really my problem, Madam. I'm a paying guest and part of what I'm paying for is off road parking for my donkey. I'm not leaving it out on the street in a neighbourhood like this. I'll come out in the morning to find it jacked up on a pile of bricks and the shoes removed.
Hester	We've had a bit of a crisis you see.
Clive	Not my problem, Madam.
Hester	You see this couple turned up looking for a place to stay.
Clive	Still not my problem, Madam.
Hester	Yes, but they were really desperate.
Clive	Desperate? I'll tell you about desperate. Me! I'm desperate. I'm desperate for my donkey to be allocated its designated parking spot in your stable. No excuses, no prevarication, no problemos.
Hester	I'm afraid there is no room in the stable. The stable is full.
Clive	Typical, just typical. This is just what I need after the day I've had. First there's a three camel pile up on the road outside of Jerusalem.
Hester	Oh dear.
Clive	Humps and legs everywhere.
Hester	How awful.
Clive	There were three foreign gentlemen having a row in the wreckage. Apparently one of the camels had shed its load and some very valuable birthday presents had been

	smashed to smithereens.
Hester	Yes, but was anyone hurt?
Clive	Well one of them was a bit upset when I criticised his driving. He said he'd been following a star. I said he should have been following the road.
Hester	Ooh, it could have been nasty.
Clive	Well it would have been if I hadn't been there to render assistance.
Hester	First aid do you mean?
Clive	Product replacement actually. I had some gold, frankincense and myrrh samples in my luggage.
Hester	That was lucky.
Clive	Luck had nothing to do with it. I'm not salesman of the year for nothing. They were hoping to replace a push-chair, changing mat and bottle steriliser.
Hester	Oh. So the presents were for a baby were they?
Clive	A baby king apparently. Born around here according to those three. Very excited about it they were.
Hester	Did they happen to say exactly where this king would be born?
Clive	Only that it would be somewhere in Bethlehem. Why?
Hester	Oh, no reason.
Clive	Now what are you going to do about my donkey situation?
Hester	I don't know. The stable really is full.
Clive	Can't you squeeze just one more little occupant into it?
Hester	I have a feeling we may be too late even for that.
Clive	But I saw a very rowdy bunch of shepherds earlier and they were heading this way. They were shouting and singing about angelic hosts. I can't leave my donkey out on the street with them about.

Hester	Whatever happens - you'll have to move it right away.
Clive	Why?
Hester	I can see someone outside looking at your donkey. They've got a bright yellow band around their head.
Clive	Do you think it's an angel?
Hester	Well it could be ... But I think, on the whole, it's more likely to be a traffic warden.

END

NIGHT COURT

Characters

Woman

Judge

Bible Background

Parable of the Unjust Judge.   Luke 18.1-8

Woman   Jesus told a story to illustrate the importance of persistence when we pray.

Judge   The city has a thousand tales to tell. This is just one of them.

Woman   There was once a judge who feared neither man nor God.

Judge   And a woman who sought to bring a case before him.

The woman approaches the judge's house.   She hammers on the door.

Woman   Coo-ee, Mr Judge. Are you there?   *(She knocks again.)* Hello? Can you hear me?   *(She knocks again.)*

Woman   Mr Judge, your honour, hello.

The judge appears, as if at a bedroom window.   He wears a night cap and is holding a candle.

Judge   *(Half asleep.)* What is it? Is there a fire?

Woman   Oh I'm sorry. Did I disturb you?

Judge   No, I had to get up. Someone was knocking at my door. What time is it?

Woman   Half past four in the morning.

Judge   What do you want?

Woman   I want you to hear my case.

Judge	Well come back during office hours and we'll see what we can do.
Woman	I've already been to your office during office hours and I was told you were too busy to see me.
Judge	Then make an appointment.
Woman	I did that. But you missed it.
Judge	I expect something urgent came up. When was it for?
Woman	Thursday afternoon.
Judge	Oh yes, I was very busy on Thursday. Very busy indeed.
Woman	I know, I saw how busy you were.
Judge	Oh, did you? About what time was that?
Woman	*(Miming a golf swing)* About FORE! You need to adjust your grip you know. That was a terrible shot on the fourteenth. You were in that bunker so long I thought you were tunnelling your way to the green.
Judge	Madam, go away and come back in the morning.
Woman	I'm not going anywhere. Now that I've found you I'm sticking with you until you hear my case.
Judge	It's the middle of the night. I don't work a night shift.
Woman	Then I'll wait. I'll wait right here.
Judge	Fine. Just keep quiet and let me sleep.

The judge vanishes from the window.

Woman	I'll just stand here and wait quietly ... I won't disturb you at all ... Don't you worry about me stood outside in the cold, in the dark, in the middle of the night. I'll be fine. I'm just a woman alone at night. Nothing to worry about. You get some sleep in your nice warm bed. Don't give me a second's thought.

The Judge reappears.

Judge	Will you keep quiet!
Woman	Sorry. Did I disturb you? You go back to bed. Get some rest.

The judge vanishes from the window.

Woman	*(Singing)* Are the stars out tonight, I don't know if it's cloudy or bright.

The judge reappears.

Judge	Shut up!
Woman	Sorry. I was just trying to keep my spirits up.

The judge vanishes from the window. The woman starts stamping her feet and noisily blowing on her hands as if to keep warm. The judge reappears.

Woman	Can't you sleep? Why don't you try a nice warm milky drink. That sometimes helps.
Judge	Please, Madam. I'm begging you.
Woman	I know what it's like to beg someone to do something. I've been begging someone (who shall remain nameless) to hear my case and give me the justice I seek. Oh yes, I can relate to the stress of crying out and not being heard.
Judge	It's the middle of the night!
Woman	You pop back into bed. I'll keep myself amused until you're ready to hear my case. You won't mind if I knit, will you? The constant clicking of my needles won't irritate you, will they?
Judge	Go away!
Woman	I've been thinking of taking up a musical instrument. Now might be a good time. Perhaps the trumpet.
Judge	Please.

61

Woman	And I've always wanted to start tap dancing but I've never had the time ... until now. Isn't it funny how sound carries at night.
Judge	All right, all right, you win. Your persistence has paid off. I'll hear your case.
Woman	What now? Are you sure it's convenient for you? I wouldn't want to keep you from something more important.
Judge	Madam, just at this moment there is nothing in the whole world more important. Now, what is the case you wish for me to hear?
Woman	It concerns my neighbour, your honour. He's ever so inconsiderate. He makes a racket all night long. And you can't imagine how annoying that can be.

END

A note about the author

Stephen Deal was a founder member of Stripes Theatre Company in 1986 and toured extensively until 1994. As the company's principal writer he wrote several revues. His play *Judas* was performed at the 1986 Edinburgh Festival 'Fringe'. The show *Pilgrims* was performed at over fifty venues in 1990 and 1991. *Gospel End* (1992 with Rob Frost) was seen throughout the U.K. The revue *Burning Questions* (written with Paul Field) was recorded for a CD (available from Kingsway) in 1993 and toured nationally in 1994, attracting total audiences of over 35,000 people. In 1996 an open air theatre event *Jubilate!* (with music by Rick Wakeman) was seen in 27 towns and combined a professional cast with local actors.

In early 1999 the show *Hopes and Dreams* for which Stephen wrote the drama and two performance poems was a sell-out at over 35 major venues. (The CD and Script and Score are available from Kingsway.)

Stephen has also written occasional material for television and radio and his sketches appear in numerous publications including the recently published *Entertaining Angels* (The Bible Society, 1998). In recent years he has co-founded The Quick Sketch Theatre Company and taken to occasional public speaking. Around 50 of his sketches are available individually by mail order from 2 Goodson House, Green Lane, Morden, Surrey, SM4 6SH (send SAE for details). He is married to Polly and lives 'on a roundabout' in South London.

Nimbus Press Titles

All our drama has been *Tried & Tested* before Church congregations or Christian audiences. If you would like our playlist please send an S.A.E. to Nimbus Press 18 Guilford Road Leicester LE2 2RB Tel: 0116 270 6318

EVEN MORE SURPRISE SKETCHES Ronald Rich   Ten pieces to challenge and inspire Christian discipleship.   ISBN 1 874424 02 0   £4.00
CELEBRATING LIGHT   Sketches for churches on the theme of 'light'. ISBN 1 874424   £2.95
SKETCHES FOR SEEKER SERVICES: 1 11 sketches presenting the Christian faith to non-Christians.   ISBN 1 874424 71 3   £2.50
SKETCHES FOR SEEKER SERVICES: 2   More short Christian drama for people on the church fringe.   ISBN 1 874424 81 0   £2.50
IS THIS YOUR LIFE? & PEARL OF GREAT PRICE   Clifford Sharp   A spoof of the TV programme. 2 ten minute plays.   ISBN 1 874424 76 4   £1.75
CALLINGS - DR LUKE'S GOSPEL OF CONCERN   Rosi MorganBarry   A cycle of 6 self-contained 10 minute plays based on Luke's gospel. ISBN 1 874424 27 6   £4.95   *Due summer 1999.*
GOOD NEWS IN BETHLEHEM Edward Bennett   Christmas. Focussing on 4 shepherds. (6m 2f 15 min) ISBN 1 874424 37 3   £1.25   *Due September 1999.*
ANGEL'S COUNSEL   Rosi MorganBarry   *Competition Winner 1997.* A Christmas Nativity/fairytale. (10parts, 30mins) ISBN 1 874424 86 1   £1.75
LOOKING FOR A KING Jonathan Curnow (Clifford Sharp)   Christmas. Two 15 min. plays - 1 biblical, 1 modern. (4parts) ISBN 1 874424 31 4   £1.75
LETS GO TO BETHLEHEM   Edward Bennett 2nd edition   Christmas plays focussing on the shepherds. (4m 15mins) ISBN 1 874424 07 1   £1.25
FULL HOUSE IN BETHLEHEM   Edward Bennett   Sequel to *Lets Go To Bethlehem.* (7m 2f 15mins) ISBN 1 874424 12 8   £1.25
THE GOLDEN AGE Clifford Sharp   Light-hearted look at environmental issues as a radio broadcast in 2192A.D. (30mins) ISBN 1 874424 10 1   £1.25
THE ROSE HAS THORNS   Edward Bennett   Modern Easter play. (3f 3m 25mins)   ISBN 1 874424 56 X   £1.25
TIME TO SPEAK   Ronald Rich   *Competition Winner 1997* Play about Pilate and Peter. (5m 2f 30mins) ISBN 1 874424 96 9   £1.75
THE PRICE OF OLIVES   Clifford Sharp   Hidden years of the youth of Jesus serves as a model for today. (5m 2f 40mins) ISBN 1 874424 46 2   £1.25
THE GOOD CHURCH GUIDE   Jonathan Curnow (Clifford Sharp) Which Church will be chosen for the new 'Good Church Guide'? (4m 3f 15mins) ISBN 1 874424 51 9   £1.25